Tarr Steps. Situated in the heart of the Exmoor countryside, Tarr Steps is an impressive 180 feet long causeway which spans the River Barle in an open wooded valley near Dulverton. This ancient clapper bridge which was probably constructed in pre-historic times consists of vast stone slabs, some of which weigh as much as five tons, laid on uprights in the bed of the stream.

Bath Abbey. There has been an abbey in Bath for more than 1000 years but the present building was founded in 1499 by the Bishop of Bath and Wells whose dream of angels climbing ladders between earth and Heaven was realised in the carvings on its intricate West Front. The abbey is also noted for its pinnacles, flying buttresses and for the majestic fan-vaulting of the interior.

Porlock. Situated in a natural bowl lying between Exmoor and the sea, Porlock is sheltered on three sides by the uplands of the Exmoor National Park. Now left inland by the retreating sea, this one-time port has a narrow, winding main street which is lined with the ancient thatch-roofed cottages which are typical of West Country architecture and particularly abundant in this area.

Exmoor. One of five ancient royal forests, Exmoor is now the smallest of Britain's National Parks covering 265 square miles. Comprising heather-clad uplands, wooded combes and wild expanses of grassy moorland the countryside is rich in wild life including hardy Exmoor ponies, red deer, an occasional otter and many types of birds from the mighty buzzard to the tiny nuthatch.

Montacute House. Now owned by the National Trust, Montacute House dates from 1601 and is one of the finest Elizabethan houses in the country. It is set in a landscaped park where the broad drive and smooth lawns are complemented by a formal garden which includes an orangery, a fig walk and a walled garden with colourful herbaceous borders and two domed pavilions.

Burnham-on-Sea. Established as a spa resort in the 19th century, Burnham-on-Sea boasts seven miles of sandy beaches. The unusual lighthouse which stands on 12 feet tall stilts in the sand was originally built in 1832 to guide ships up the Bristol Channel and into Bridgwater Bay. Out of service for 25 years, it was recommissioned in 1993 to replace another shore-based lighthouse.

Dunster. The countryside of West Somerset is enriched with attractive thatched, colour-washed cottages. This superb example, known as Rose Cottage, stands surrounded by beautiful wooded countryside on the northern edge of Exmoor. In addition to its octagonal Yarn Market this unspoilt little town boasts a fine 15th century priory church and is overlooked by its Norman castle.

Cheddar. Situated at the foot of the gorge, the village of Cheddar has a straggling main street with the parish church at one end and an ancient preachers' cross later converted into a market centre for travelling merchants. Home of the famous Cheddar Cheese, which was declared by Henry II to be the "best cheese in England", the village is overshadowed by the impressive Lion Rock.

Oare Church. The Exmoor hamlet of Oare is at the heart of the Lorna Doone country which features in R. D. Blackmore's novel and it was on the altar steps of tiny Oare Church, during her marriage to John Ridd, that Lorna was shot by Carver Doone. The church contains a number of interesting items including a font bowl which dates from Norman times and an Elizabethan chalice.

Clifton. Situated on the downs above Bristol, Clifton is known for its fine Regency crescents and Georgian terraces many of which were built by prosperous merchants and shipowners when Bristol's fortunes as a port were at their height. Handsome Royal York Crescent, which stands on a raised causeway, is nearly a quarter of a mile long and claims to be the largest crescent in England.

East Quantoxhead. Situated in an idyllic corner of Somerset where the Quantock Hills roll down towards the sea, this tranquil village has belonged to the Luttrell family, owners of Dunster Castle, for over 800 years. The duckpond, surrounded by a cluster of attractive old cottages, forms the centre of the village and Court House, the Luttrells' fine 17th century home stands nearby.

Brympton d'Evercy. Situated some two miles west of Yeovil, this splendid mansion is built of local Ham Hill limestone and incorporates several architectural styles. The west front dates from Tudor times but the house has been restored and rebuilt over the centuries and the attractive south front, overlooking the lake, is late 17th century. The stables house a museum of rural life.

Minehead. Overlooking the Bristol Channel is the popular resort of Minehead, much frequented by holiday makers. Once it was an important port but the harbour began to silt up in the late 18th century and now provides a small but attractive haven for fishermen and pleasure boats. Beneath the quaint Old Town which clings to the hillside there is also a fine mile-long curving stretch of sand.

Allerford. Situated on the northern edge of Exmoor picturesque Allerford is an ancient village recorded in the Domesday Book. A centre for some fine woodland walks, it has an unusual thatched school house and a number of quaint cottages built of local red sandstone stand beside the attractive, double-arched medieval pack-horse bridge which is paved with cobbles.

Ashton Mill. Once one of more than 50 mills in Somerset, Ashton Tower Mill stands at Chapel Allerton some five miles south-west of Cheddar Gorge. It dates from the 19th century and ceased to work as a grist mill in the 1920s. With its triangular gable, one of the simplest forms of cap, it has now been completely restored and is one of the finest mills surviving in the West Country.

Taunton. A major centre of the wool trade for 500 years and one of the most important livestock markets in the West Country, Taunton is situated at the heart of the fertile Vale of Taunton Deane. Vivary Park, entered through an ornate Victorian decorative gateway, stands on land that once belonged to a priory and takes its name from the monks' fishpond, or *vivarium*.

Glastonbury Tor. This conspicuous landmark which rises abruptly from the surrounding Somerset levels reaches a height of 521 feet and is capped by the 13th century tower of St. Michael's Church, built on the site of an earlier Saxon church. The view from the top encompasses many of the county's landmarks including Wells Cathedral, the Mendips and the Quantock Hills.

Tintinhull. Among the stately homes of South Somerset is the delightful 17th century gabled farmhouse of Tintinhull near Yeovil. The formal gardens are divided by walls and hedges into six areas each with its own distinctive theme including a kitchen garden where traditional vegetables and fruit trees are grown and an attractive Pool Garden with a canal flanked by colourful borders.

Clifton Suspension Bridge. From Clifton there is a spectacular view of the strikingly beautiful Avon Gorge spanned by Brunel's fine suspension bridge. Stretching 702 feet from pier to pier and suspended a breathtaking 245 feet above the gorge, the bridge was described by Brunel as "my first child, my darling" but it was not completed until 1864, five years after his death.

Selworthy. Situated on the wooded hillside below Selworthy Beacon, the delightful little village of Selworthy looks out across the lush valley to Dunkery and the Exmoor hills. Here several of the fine white-walled thatched cottages which are abundant in this part of Somerset are grouped in leafy lanes around the magnificent, largely 14th century Church of All Saints.

Wells Cathedral. England's smallest city, which lies at the foot of the Mendip Hills, is famous for its magnificent 13th century cathedral. This serene and beautiful building was the first English cathedral built entirely in the Gothic style. It is seen here from the moat which surrounds the Bishop's Palace, one of the oldest inhabited houses in England dating in part from 1206.

Bath. Famous for the mineral springs which made it a celebrated spa, Bath is one of Britain's oldest and best-preserved cities. Although the healing powers of the waters were recognised much earlier it was the Romans who built the elaborate baths and the Great Bath itself, which was not rediscovered until the late 19th century, retains its original Roman lead lining intact.

Dunster. Standing in the centre of the High Street, a broad and dignified thoroughfare lined by Tudor houses and ancient shops, is picturesque Dunster's eight-sided Yarn Market. This distinctive building dates from the time when Dunster was an important wool market and weaving centre. It was damaged during the Civil War but later repaired by the Luttrells of Dunster Castle.

Malmsmead. Although it is difficult to identify all the fictional locations referred to in *Lorna Doone*, the Badgworthy Water which joins the Lyn River at Malmsmead will always be associated with Blackmore's novel. Lorna Doone Farm is a well-known landmark which stands beside the Badgworthy Water where it is crossed by Malmsmead Bridge and the adjacent ford.

Isle Abbotts. In a region of remote villages and small market towns this picturesque village is situated in low-lying countryside beside the River Isle not far from Taunton. Ancient cottages with their delightful gardens stand beside the parish church which has a fine carved perpendicular tower and is one of a group of three churches in the area which are considered among the finest in Somerset.

Cheddar Gorge. With its 450 feet high, wooded limestone cliffs rising almost vertically above the twisting road, Cheddar Gorge is one of England's great natural tourist attractions. Extending for about two miles it was probably once the course of a river bed and beneath the rocks there are spectacular caverns in which underground rivers and petrified waterfalls can be seen.

Porlock. The picturesque old Ship Inn is one of the best-known features of the village of Porlock and in it a chimney-corner is dedicated to the memory of poet Robert Southey who penned one of his sonnets here. The road to Lynmouth runs through the High Street and up the famous, and now by-passed, Porlock Hill known for its hairpin bends and steep gradients.

West Somerset Railway. A sandy beach backed by a strip of shingle runs all the way from Blue Anchor to Minehead, making this a popular area with holiday-makers. Amidst beautiful coastal scenery, the West Somerset Railway runs along Blue Anchor Bay to Watchet before turning inland. The first train on this privately operated route ran in 1976, five years after British Rail closed the line.

Weston-super-Mare. Known for its superb sands, gardens, promenades and other amusements, Weston-super-Mare is one of the finest and most popular of the West Country holiday resorts with views across Weston Bay to the distant Welsh hills. The Grand Pier, larger and newer of Weston's two piers, was completed in 1904 and provides many traditional seaside entertainments.

Bristol. Once an important sea port, the city of Bristol grew up around its harbour on the River Avon and derived its prosperity largely from shipping wool and from the importation of tobacco, sugar and wines. The impressive Floating Harbour, completed in 1809, is still at the heart of the city and Bristol's seafaring traditions are celebrated in the Maritime Heritage Centre.

Barrington Court. This fine Tudor mansion situated north of Ilminster was built between 1514 and 1520 and is now owned by the National Trust. The beautiful gardens which were laid out in the 1920s show the influence of Gertrude Jekyll notably in the Lily Garden where the red and yellow plants surrounding the central pool blend with the mellow brick walls of the house.

Norton St. Philip. The impressive 15th century George Inn stands in the village of Norton St. Philip five miles north of Frome and is one of the finest examples of its kind in the whole of England. Supporters of the ill-fated Monmouth Rebellion were incarcerated in a dungeon which now forms part of the inn and other famous patrons include Samuel Pepys, Oliver Cromwell and Judge Jeffreys.

Doone Valley. From the wilds of Exmoor, the lovely Badgworthy Water flows down through the valley that was immortalised in R. D. Blackmore's famous novel Lorna Doone as the home of the infamous Doones of Badgworthy. The author built his story upon local legends and it is probable that there was an actual band of outlaws who terrorised this area in the 17th century.

Glastonbury Abbey. Connected in legend with both Joseph of Arimathea and King Arthur, Glastonbury is said to be the cradle of British Christianity. The Abbey is believed to have been founded in the 4th or 5th century as a Celtic monastery but the great Abbey Church was added between 1184 and 1303. It was allowed to fall into ruins after the Dissolution of the Monasteries.

Porlock Weir. The picturesque little seaside village of Porlock Weir lies at the west side of Porlock Bay surrounded by fine wooded cliff scenery. The tiny harbour, overlooked by colour-washed cottages and old inns, was once busy with coasters carrying timber to South Wales in exchange for coal. It is still a popular port of call although today it is used mainly by pleasure craft.

Bossington. Somerset contains numerous beautiful stone-built villages where many of the farmhouses and cottages date from the 16th to the 18th centuries. The delightful village of Bossington lies at the seaward end of the Vale of Porlock, sheltered beneath 800 feet high Bossington Hill. This lovely old thatched cottage with its round chimneys is typical of many found in this area.

Front cover: Minehead – Back cover: Glastonbury Tor